WALKING WITH HENRY
BASED ON THE LIFE AND WORKS OF HENRY DAVID THOREAU

BY THOMAS LOCKER

Fulcrum Publishing
Golden, Colorado

The Thoreau Institute at Walden Woods
Lincoln, Massachusetts

Dedicated to my son, Greg, the first walker
of the Appalachian Trail from Georgia to Maine
in the year 2000.

Fulcrum Publishing
Golden, Colorado

The Thoreau Institute at Walden Woods
Lincoln, Massachusetts

Library of Congress Cataloging-in-Publication Data

Locker, Thomas, 1937–
Walking with Henry : based on the life and works of Henry David
Thoreau / Thomas Locker.
p. cm.
Summary: Introduces philosopher, writer, and environmentalist Henry
David Thoreau, using selections from his own writings and an imaginary
journey into the wilderness.
ISBN 1-55591-355-5 (Hardcover)
1. Thoreau, Henry David, 1817–1862—Juvenile literature. 2.
Wilderness areas—Juvenile literature. 3. Walking—Juvenile literature.
4. Nature—Juvenile literature. [1. Thoreau, Henry David, 1817–1862. 2.
Authors, American. 3. Naturalists. 4. Wilderness areas. 5. Walking. 6.
Nature.] I. Title.
PS3053 .L58 2002
818'.309—dc21
2002003881

Printed and bound in China

0 9 8 7 6 5 4 3 2

Design by Nancy Duncan-Cashman

Fulcrum Publishing
16100 Table Mountain Parkway, Suite 300, Golden, Colorado 80403
(800) 992-2908 • (303) 277-1623
www.fulcrum-books.com

"In Wildness is the preservation of the world . . ."

"How many a man has dated a new era in his
life from the reading of a book!"

—Henry David Thoreau

Once there was a nature writer

Named Henry David Thoreau

Who lived in Concord, Massachusetts,

And loved to walk in the wilderness.

One day Henry

Cut down a sapling for a walking stick.

Leaving the cares of civilization behind

He followed a path by the river.

The path ended at the edge of the wilderness.

Henry set up his tent and

Peeled the bark from his walking stick

As the lingering sunset faded and

Darkness covered the land.

At first light he entered the pathless wilderness.

The air was filled with the smells of plants

Growing and decaying.

Listening to the sounds of animals,

Henry studied the moss and the ferns, the trees and the flowers,

Walking carefully to avoid snakes.

The farther he went from civilization

The happier he became.

At the top of a waterfall, Henry took out

His carving knife and whittled his stick.

Time seemed to disappear.

Startled by the hooting night owls,

Henry sat up in his tent, then fell asleep

Listening to the sound of falling water.

When he awoke, the grass was covered with

Morning dew. It looked like a mirror

Broken into a thousand fragments

Wildly reflecting the full blaze of the rising sun.

Through the glare and mist, Henry was

Astonished to see a large moose

Entering the forest.

Hoping for a closer look

Henry followed the moose tracks.

They led to a sparkling lake

At the foot of a gigantic mountain.

It was like a dream of paradise.

He wondered what he would see

From the mountaintop.

Using his sturdy walking stick

Henry struggled up the mountain

Passing huge rocks that seemed to

Have been dropped from an unseen quarry.

Bone tired, Henry reached the summit

As the last light of day faded into night.

The moon rose silently.

Millions of stars appeared in the endless sky.

Huddling close to the warmth

Of his small crackling campfire

Henry carved the handle of his staff

Until it fit perfectly in his hand.

At dawn Henry picked up his stick.

It wasn't too short or too long.

It wasn't too thick or too thin.

Like the wilderness, it was the way it should be.

Henry looked out over the world

And then descended into the rising mist.

As he started home, the woods became dark.

Trees began to sway in a wild howling wind.

Henry heard the fierce drumbeat of

Rain pounding on the roof of the forest.

Soon both Henry and the wilderness were soaked.

When the storm ended, everything became silent.

A brown wood thrush sang and another answered.

Henry listened to the sound of the creek filling

And recognized familiar rocks, trees and animals.

It was like meeting old friends or even family.

Enjoying the fellowship, Henry sauntered

Toward the light streaming in from

The edge of the wilderness.

The warm sun on his back

Was like a gentle herdsman leading him home.

When he found the path by the river

His heart was filled with a love of the world.

Near his home, he planted an acorn in case

He would ever need another walking stick.

But his walking stick, shaped and tested

By the wilderness, lasted for many years.

The acorn grew into a wild and noble oak.

Henry David Thoreau's words about wildness

Still echo across the land.

THOREAU ON WILDERNESS

Henry David Thoreau was a walker who spent several hours each day wandering in the woods. When he returned from his walks, he wrote some of the finest things ever written about nature. Here are a few selections of his words.

Our village life would stagnate if it were not for the unexplored forests and meadows which surround it. We need the tonic of wildness.... We can never have enough of nature.

A man is rich in proportion to the number of things which he can afford to let alone.

I believe in the forest, and in the meadow, and in the night in which the corn grows.

The world is but canvas to our imaginations.

If one advances confidently in the direction of his dreams, and endeavors to live the life which he has imagined, he will meet with a success unexpected in common hours.

If I am not I, who will be?

I think that I cannot preserve my health and spirits, unless I spend four hours a day at least—and it is commonly more than that—sauntering through the woods and over the fields, absolutely free from all worldly engagement.

In the society of many men, or in the midst of what is called success, I find my life of no account, and my spirits rapidly fail.... But when I hear only a rustling oak leaf, or the faint metallic cheep of a tree sparrow, for variety in my winter walk, my life becomes content and sweet as the kernel of a nut.

Nowadays almost all man's improvements, so called, as the building of houses, and the cutting down of the forest and all large trees, simply deform the landscape, and makes it more and more tame and cheap.

A town is saved, not more by the righteous men in it than by the woods and swamps that surround it.

I seek acquaintance with nature, to know her moods and manners.

We must have infinite faith in each other.... There is the same ground for faith now that ever there was. It needs only a little love in you who complain so to ground it on.

We are as much as we see. Faith is sight and knowledge.

In short, all good things are wild and free.

I had prepared myself to speak a word now for nature—for absolute Freedom and Wildness, as contrasted with a freedom and culture simply civil—to regard man as an inhabitant, or a part and parcel of nature—rather than a member of society.